A New True Book

JUPITER

By Dennis B. Fradin

CHILDRENS PRESS®

CHICAGO

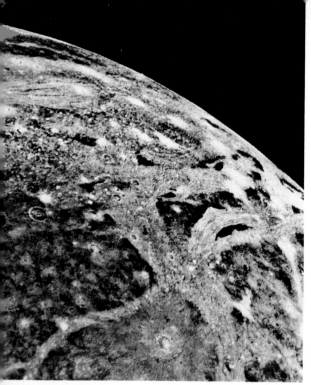

PHOTO CREDITS

Courtesy American Petroleum Institute—6

Historical Pictures Service, Chicago—19 (2 photos), 23, 28

NASA—5, 11 (right), 12 (right), 31, 33 (left), 35, 36, 40, 45

NASA-JET PROPULSION LAB—Cover, 2, 9, 10, 11 (left), 15, 30, 39 (2 photos), 43

North Wind Picture Archives—21

© James Oberg—33 (right)

Photri—12 (left), 14, 16, 25 (4 photos), 27

Tony Stone Worldwide-Click/Chicago—DOUG ARMOND, 7

Cover—Jupiter. Moons Io, Europa, Ganymede, Callisto

For my beautiful sister, Lori Fradin Polster, who likes Jupiter because it is so big and has a Great Red Spot

Ganymede is one of Jupiter's moons.

Library of Congress Cataloging-in-Publication Data

Fradin, Dennis B.
    Jupiter / by Dennis B. Fradin.
        p.   cm. — (A New True book)
    Includes index.
    Summary: Discusses the giant planet, how it was named, and the information astronomers have gathered about it.
    ISBN 0-516-01173-1
    1. Jupiter (Planet)—Juvenile literature.
[1. Jupiter (Planet)]   I. Title.
QB661.F73   1989
523.4′5—dc20
                                        89-9983
                                        CIP
                                        AC

TABLE OF CONTENTS

OUR SUN IS A STAR

On a clear night you can see hundreds of stars. There are red stars and yellow stars. There are white stars and blue stars. Stars are giant balls of hot, glowing gas. There are many, many millions of stars in space.

The nighttime stars are in the sky during the daytime, too. But we cannot see them during the day because our sky

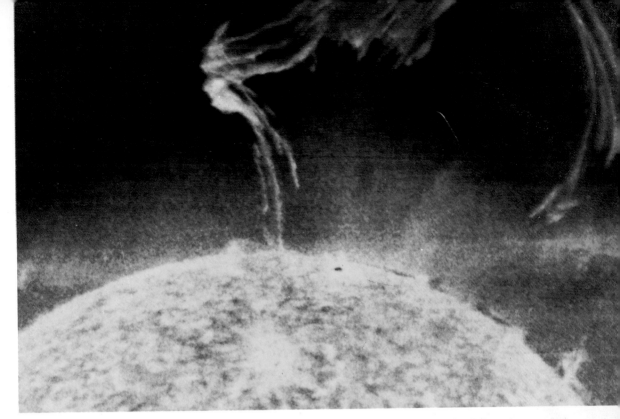

The Sun is a star.

is too bright. A star that is special to us lights up our daytime sky. We call this star the Sun.

We could not survive without the Sun. The Sun provides living things with

the light and heat they
need. Yet, for a star, the
Sun is really about average
in size and heat. It just
seems to be the biggest
and hottest star because it
is the closest star to us.

THE SUN'S PLANETS

The stars seem to twinkle, or blink, as we look at them. This happens because our planet's air plays tricks with starlight. On many nights one or

Stars are giant balls of hot, glowing gas.

more starlike objects that don't twinkle can also be seen in the sky. They are planets.

The planets are much smaller than the Sun. They orbit, or move around, the Sun and get their heat and light from the Sun. The reason the planets don't twinkle is that they don't have light of their own. The planets reflect, or bounce back, the light from the Sun. Our air plays less tricks with the planets' reflected light than it does with starlight.

The Sun has at least nine planets that orbit it. Mercury is the closest planet to the Sun. It is usually lost in the Sun's

Mercury

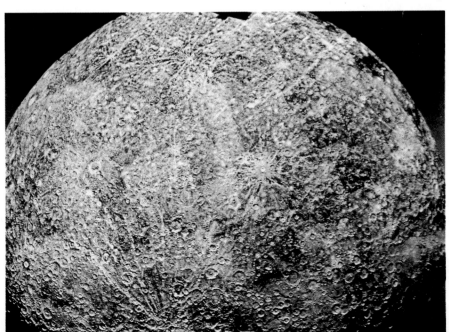

glare. But on about thirty-
five days a year, bright
orange-yellow Mercury can
be seen near sunset or
sunrise. Venus, the second
planet, is the brightest
object in our sky besides
the Sun and the Moon.
Bright white Venus can
often be seen after sunset
or before sunrise.

Venus

Mars

Earth

The third planet is our home, Earth. To see it, all you need do is look down at the ground! Mars is the fourth planet from the Sun. It is nicknamed the "red planet" because of its color. If you see a red heavenly body that does not twinkle, it is Mars.

11

Jupiter

Saturn

Jupiter, the fifth planet, can also be seen with just our eyes. Jupiter is usually the second-brightest planet, after Venus. It is yellow-white in color. Saturn, the sixth planet, looks much like Jupiter. But it is not quite as bright and it is a bit more yellowish.

Uranus, the seventh planet, is very dim. To see it with just your eyes, you must be in a very dark place with clean air. You must also know exactly where to look. There are special maps that show where the planets are at any given time.

A telescope is needed to see the remaining two planets, Neptune and Pluto. Astronomers use telescopes to study the stars and

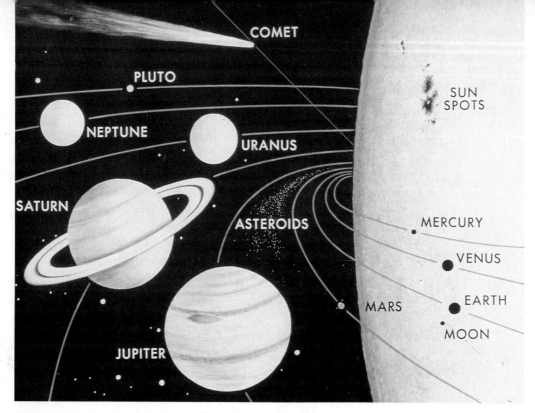

The Sun is the center of our Solar System.

planets. The Sun and its
nine planets are the main
members of the Solar
System. The Solar System
is the Sun's "family" of
objects. The moons are
other major members of

Jupiter and its four largest moons—Io, Europa, Ganymede, Callisto

the Solar System. Moons
are objects that orbit every
planet but Mercury and
Venus.

Probably millions of
other stars also have

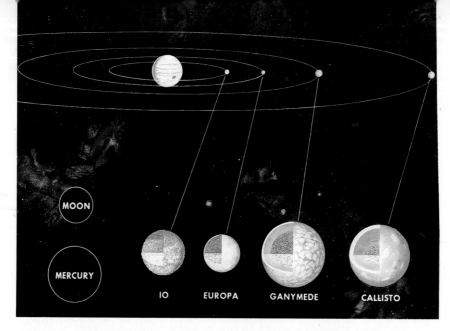

MOON

MERCURY

IO EUROPA GANYMEDE CALLISTO

The drawing shows the orbit of Jupiter's four largest moons
and their size as compared to Mercury and the Earth's moon.

planets. But they are too
far away for us to learn
much about them. We
know a great deal about
Jupiter and our Solar
System's other planets,
though. This knowledge
was slowly gathered over
thousands of years.

16

ANCIENT PEOPLE AND JUPITER

Ancient people did not understand the Solar System. They thought that the Sun and the planets circled Earth. This is not so. The Sun and the planets only seem to circle our sky because our Earth is spinning. The fact is, Earth and the other planets orbit the Sun.

The ancients also thought that the planets were gods. For example, many ancient peoples thought the brightest planet was a lovely goddess. The Babylonians (of what is now Iraq) named the bright white planet after Ishtar. She was the mother of their gods. The Romans called it Venus, after their goddess of love and beauty. We still call it Venus today.

The bright yellow-white

planet seemed like a king to the ancients. This may have been because of the slow, stately way it moved. The Babylonians called the planet Marduk, after the king of their gods. The ancient Romans called it Jupiter, after the king of their gods. We still call it Jupiter today.

Venus (far left) was the Roman goddess of love and beauty. Jupiter (left) was the king of all the Roman gods.

COPERNICUS LEARNS THE TRUTH

For thousands of years, people believed that the planets orbit Earth. The Polish astronomer Nicolaus Copernicus (1473-1543) discovered the truth. Copernicus said that the other planets do not orbit Earth. Instead, Earth and all the other planets orbit the Sun.

Copernicus also learned some other basic facts

Nicolaus Copernicus was the first astronomer to understand that all the planets orbit the Sun.

about the planets. He learned that Jupiter takes almost twelve earth-years to orbit the Sun. This means that a year on Jupiter would be almost twelve earth-years long.

And he figured out that
Jupiter is about 500
million miles from the Sun.
This makes it about five
times as far from the Sun
as our Earth is.

Copernicus explained how
the Solar System really
works. But people still knew
nothing about conditions on
the planets. Our eyes alone
cannot see details on the
planets. Something stronger
than the eye was needed
to show those details.

JUPITER THROUGH EARLY TELESCOPES

Galileo used a telescope to study the stars and the planets.

The first telescope was made about 400 years ago, in about 1608. Galileo (1564-1642) of Italy was the first famous astronomer to use a telescope. Galileo

discovered that the Moon
has mountains. He learned
that the Milky Way is
made of millions of stars.
In 1610 he made a big
discovery about Jupiter.

Galileo saw four little
bodies near Jupiter. Night
after night he watched
these little objects. They
were orbiting Jupiter! This
meant they were moons of
Jupiter. They were the first
moons beyond our own
Moon to be discovered.

Voyager photographs of Io (top left),
Callisto (top right), Ganymede (left),
and Europa (above)

Each year more powerful
telescopes were built. They
provided better views of
many objects, including
Jupiter. Around 1660
astronomers first saw the

dark belts that cross Jupiter. And in 1664 the English scientist Robert Hooke saw a big spot on Jupiter. It became known as the Great Red Spot because of its color. Jupiter's belts, Great Red Spot, and four main moons can be seen in the small telescopes of today's amateur astronomers.

The planets all rotate, or spin. The time it takes for a planet to rotate once is the length of its day.

Voyager photograph of Jupiter taken
at a distance of 22 million miles

The day on Earth is about
twenty-four hours long. In
1665 a Frenchman, Jean
Dominique Cassini (1625-
1712), timed Jupiter's

Jean Dominique Cassini was a French astronomer.

rotation period. Cassini learned that Jupiter rotates once in a little under ten hours. Thus, Jupiter's day is just under ten hours long.

BETTER TELESCOPES
SHOW MORE OF JUPITER

Bigger and better telescopes were built between the late 1600s and the 1900s. They slowly revealed some of Jupiter's secrets. For one thing, more moons of Jupiter were discovered. By 1951 Jupiter was known to have at least twelve moons.

Jupiter is covered by clouds.

Early astronomers had known that Jupiter was the biggest planet. Little by little they came closer to measuring its exact size. By the mid-1900s Jupiter was known to have a

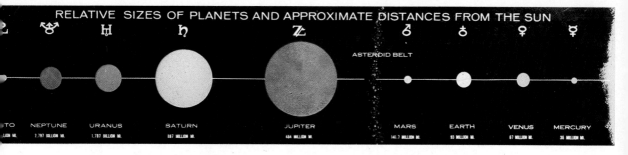

diameter of about 88,700
miles. Jupiter is so big
that about 1,400 Earths
could fit inside it. Jupiter
is called the "giant planet"
because of its size.

When we view Jupiter,
we are not seeing its
surface. We are seeing
clouds. By the mid-1900s
astronomers knew that
Jupiter's clouds were
made of poisonous gases.

31

However, by 1970 many questions about Jupiter remained. What was the Great Red Spot? What were the conditions in Jupiter's clouds? What was the giant planet's surface like beneath the clouds? What were the conditions on Jupiter's moons? Telescopes were unable to answer such questions. A closer view of Jupiter was needed to find the answers.

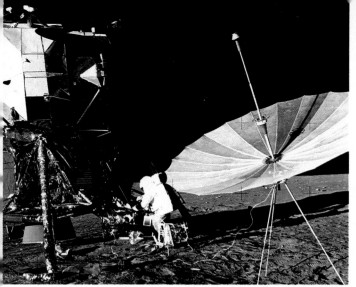

Apollo XII (above) and *Sputnik I* (right)

SPACE PROBES APPROACH JUPITER

The space age began in October, 1957, when Russia launched the first artificial satellite, *Sputnik I.* Twelve years later, in 1969, the United States landed two men on the Moon. This was the first visit by people to another heavenly body.

The planets were too distant for people to visit as yet. Instead, the United States and Russia began sending space probes to the planets. The space probes carried no people. But they carried scientific instruments that could send photos and data back to Earth.

In spring of 1972 the United States sent the

Pioneer X was launched on March 3, 1972. On June 13, 1983, it was 2.8 billion miles away from the Sun. It continued its journey and is now beyond our Solar System.

Pioneer X probe toward Jupiter. In late 1973 it came within about 80,000 miles of the giant planet.

35

Pioneer X sent the first close-up pictures of Jupiter to Earth. A year later, a second probe, *Pioneer-Saturn*, came within 25,000 miles of Jupiter.

The Pioneer probes found the Great Red Spot

Photograph of Jupiter's Great Red Spot

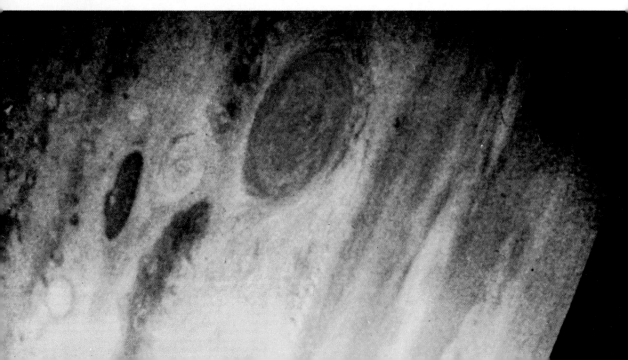

to be much like a huge hurricane. It is so big that several Earths could fit across it. The Pioneer probes found that Jupiter may have little or no solid surface. The planet may be all—or almost all—gas and liquids. They also took Jupiter's temperature. At its cloud tops Jupiter is very cold—minus 235°F. But lower down, Jupiter is hot. About 600 miles below the cloud tops, Jupiter's temperature is more than 6,000°F.

THE VOYAGERS

In late summer of 1977, the United States launched two more probes toward Jupiter, *Voyager I* and *Voyager II*. The Voyager mission was to study Jupiter and then Saturn, Uranus, and Neptune.

Voyager I neared Jupiter in early 1979. *Voyager II* neared the giant planet in mid-1979. The two Voyagers revealed some surprises about Jupiter.

Voyager spacecraft (above) photographed Jupiter and sent information back to Earth about the planet's cloud movements (right).

Many storms swirl Jupiter's clouds around. The winds in these storms reach 250 miles an hour. Huge lightning bolts were also seen in Jupiter's clouds.

Saturn had once been thought to be the only

A ring has been discovered around Jupiter.

planet with rings. In 1977 Uranus had been found to have rings. The Voyager probes found that Jupiter has a ring too! Just a few miles thick, Jupiter's ring is made of tiny particles.

The Voyagers also found several more moons of Jupiter. The giant planet has at least sixteen moons. Only Saturn, with over twenty, is known to have more moons than Jupiter.

The Voyagers learned a great deal about Jupiter's four biggest moons. Because it was Galileo who discovered them, they are called the Galilean moons. Their names are Callisto,

Europa, Ganymede, and Io.
The Voyagers learned that
Callisto is covered with
craters. Europa is very
smooth. Ganymede has
many valleys and many
mountains. But Io provided
the biggest surprise of all.

On March 9, 1979, the
scientist Linda Morabito
was studying a Voyager
photograph of Io in a
California laboratory. She
spotted a volcano erupting
on Io in the picture! This
was the first active

A huge erupting volcano was discovered on Io.

volcano discovered beyond
Earth. Later a few other
active volcanoes were
found on Io. Perhaps dust
from Io's volcanoes went
into making Jupiter's ring.

JUPITER STILL HAS MANY MYSTERIES

No one has seen what Jupiter is like beneath its clouds. Does Jupiter have a solid surface? Or is it all gases and liquids?

Like Saturn, Jupiter gives off more heat than it gets from the Sun. What is the source of this heat? How did the Great Red Spot form? Why is there just one spot and not many? Why does Jupiter have so many moons?

Astronomers still have many questions about Jupiter, the giant planet.

In the future, more probes will be launched to search for the answers. Solving Jupiter's mysteries may help us learn how the whole Solar System, including our Earth, was formed.

45

FACTS ABOUT JUPITER

Average Distance from Sun —
About 484 million miles

Closest Approach to Earth —
About 390 million miles

Diameter — About 88,700 miles

Length of Day — A little under
10 hours

Length of Year — About 12
earth-years

Temperatures — At its cloud
tops, Jupiter is -235° F;
but below the outer clouds,
Jupiter is very hot

Atmosphere — Hydrogen,
helium, methane, ammonia,
and several other
substances

Number of Moons — At least
16

*Weight of an Object on
Jupiter That Would Weigh
100 Pounds on Earth —* 264
pounds

*Average Speed as Jupiter
Orbits the Sun —* About 8
miles per second

WORDS YOU SHOULD KNOW

amateur(AM • iht • cher) — a person who does something just for
fun
ancient(AIN • shent) — very old
astronomer(ast • RAH • nih • mer) — a person who studies stars,
planets, and other heavenly bodies
atmosphere(AT • muss • feer) — the gases surrounding some
heavenly bodies
crater(KRAY • ter) — a bowl-shaped hollow on a heavenly body
Galilean moons(gal • ih • LAY • in MOONZ) — Jupiter's four
biggest moons, which Galileo discovered
Great Red Spot(GRATE REHD SPAHT) — a huge hurricane-like
storm on Jupiter

heavenly body(HEV•vin•lee BAH•dee)—an object in space, such as a star, planet, or moon

Jupiter(JOO•pih•ter)—the fifth planet from the Sun

million(MILL•yun)—a thousand thousand (1,000,000)

moon(MOON)—a natural object that orbits a planet; Jupiter has at least 16 moons

orbit(OR•biht)—the path a heavenly body takes when it moves around another heavenly body

planet(PLAN•it)—a large object that orbits a star; the Sun has nine planets

rotate(ROH•tait)—to spin

satellite(SAT•ihl•ite)—a body that revolves around a heavenly body; a moon is a natural satellite, while *Sputnik I* was an artificial satellite

Solar System(SOH•ler SISS•tim)—the Sun and its "family" of objects

space probe(SPAISS PROHB)—an unmanned spacecraft sent to study heavenly bodies

star(STAHR)—a giant ball of hot, glowing gases

Sun(SUHN)—the yellow star that is the closest star to Earth

telescope(TEL•ih•skohp)—an instrument that makes distant objects look closer

volcano(vahl•KAY•noh)—an opening in the ground through which material erupts; a mountain, also called a volcano, builds up around the opening

INDEX

About the Author

Dennis B. Fradin attended Northwestern University on a partial creative scholarship and was graduated in 1967. His previous books include the Young People's Stories of Our States series for Childrens Press, and Bad Luck Tony for Prentice-Hall. In the New True Book series Dennis has written about astronomy, farming, comets, archaeology, movies, space colonies, the space lab, explorers, and pioneers. He is married and the father of three children.